M000160142

ROCK OF AGES

SHEET MUSIC SELECTIONS FROM THE MOTION PICTURE

Alfred

Produced by
Alfred Music Publishing Co., Inc.
P.O. Box 10003
Van Nuys, CA 91410-0003

alfred.com

Printed in USA.

ISBN-10: 0-7390-9160-3
ISBN-13: 978-0-7390-9160-9

 Alfred Cares. Contents printed on 100% recycled paper, except pages 1–4 which are printed on 60% recycled paper.

PARADISE CITY

Words and Music by
W. AXL ROSE, SLASH, IZZY STRADLIN,
DUFF McKAGAN and STEVEN ADLER

6

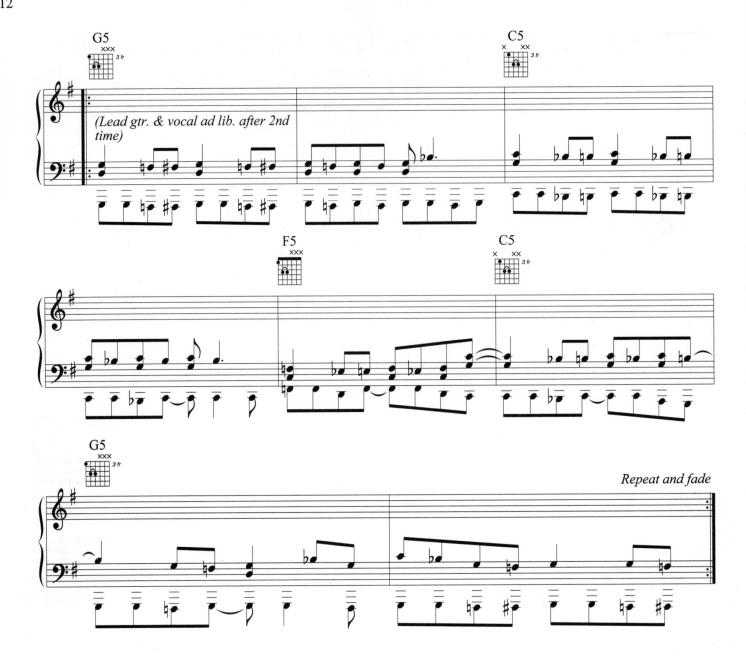

Additional Lyrics

2. Ragz to richez, or so they say.
   Ya gotta keep pushin' for the fortune and fame.
   It's all a gamble when it's just a game.
   Ya treat it like a capital crime.
   Everybody's doin' their time. *(To Chorus)*

3. Strapped in the chair of the city's gas chamber,
   Why I'm here I can't quite remember.
   The surgeon general says it's hazarous to breathe.
   I'd have anothe cigarette but I can't see.
   Tell me who ya gonna believe? *(To Chorus)*

4. Captain America's been torn a part.
   Now he's a court jester with a broken heart.
   He said, "Turn me around and take me back to the start."
   I must be losin' my mind. "Are you blind?"
   I've seen it all a million times. *(To Chorus)*

SISTER CHRISTIAN/JUST LIKE PARADISE/ NOTHIN' BUT A GOOD TIME

Moderately slow rock ♩ = 92

(with pedal)

Verse:
"Sister Christian"
Words and Music by
KELLY KEAGY

Sis-ter Chris-tian, oh, the time has come,____ and you know that you're the

Chorus:

mo-tor-ing. What's your price for flight___ in find-ing Mis-ter Right?___

___ You'll be al-right to-night.___

Driving rock ♩ = 144

"Just Like Paradise"
Words and Music by
DAVID LEE ROTH and BRETT TUGGLE

18

Driving rock, a little slower ♩ = 132
"Nothin' But A Good Time"
Words and Music by
BOBBY DALL, BRETT MICHAELS, BRUCE JOHANNESSON and RIKKI ROCKETT

Verse:

1. Not a dime, I can't pay my___ rent. I can bare-ly make it through the week.
(2.) spend my mon-ey on wom-en and wine, but I could-n't tell you where I

Sat - ur-day night,___ I'd like to make my___ girl,___ but right
spent last night.___ I'm real-ly sor - ry 'bout the shape I'm in.___ I just

*How can I___ re-sist?_____ Ain't look-in' for noth - in' but a good_*

___ time, and it don't___ get bet - ter than this."___

To Coda ⊕

(Guitar solo ad lib....

JUKE BOX HERO / I LOVE ROCK AND ROLL

Moderate rock ♩ = 96

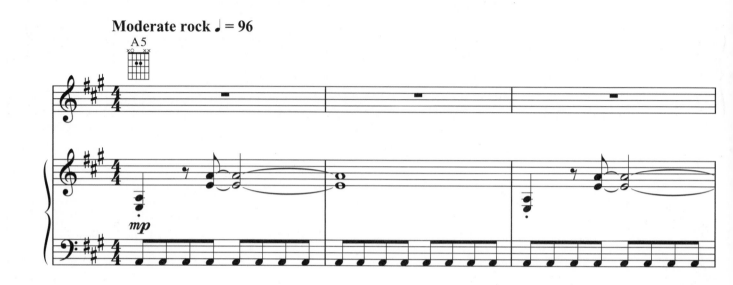

Verse 1:
"Juke Box Hero"
Words and Music by
MICK JONES and LOU GRAMM

1. Bought a beat-up six - string in a sec-ond-hand

store. Did-n't know how to play it, but I knew for sure that one gui-tar_

Chorus:
"I Love Rock 'N' Roll"
Words and Music by
ALAN MERRILL and JAKE HOOKER

make it to the top___ and say: I love rock and roll,___ so

put an-oth-er dime in the juke-box, ba-by. I love rock and roll,___ so

come and take your time and dance with me. 2. In a town with-out a

Verse 2:

name, in a heav-y down-pour, thought I passed my own shad-ow by the back-stage

HIT ME WITH YOUR BEST SHOT

Words and Music by
EDDIE SCHWARTZ

Moderate rock ♩ = 120

Verses 1 & 2 (Sing 1st and 2nd time only):

1. Well, you're a real tough cook - ie with a long his - to - ry of
(2.) come on with a come on; you don't fight fair.

Verse 3 (Sing 3rd time only):

(3.) real tough cook - ie with a long his - to - ry of

break - ing lit - tle hearts like the one in me. That's_ O. K., let's see_
But that's O K. See if I___ care._ Knock_ me down, it's all_

break - ing lit - tle hearts like the one in me. Be - fore I put an - oth - er notch_ in my

Hit Me With Your Best Shot - 4 - 1

Hit Me With Your Best Shot - 4 - 4

WAITING FOR A GIRL LIKE YOU

Words and Music by
MICK JONES and LOU GRAMM

To Coda

MORE THAN WORDS/HEAVEN

Moderately slow ♩ = 92

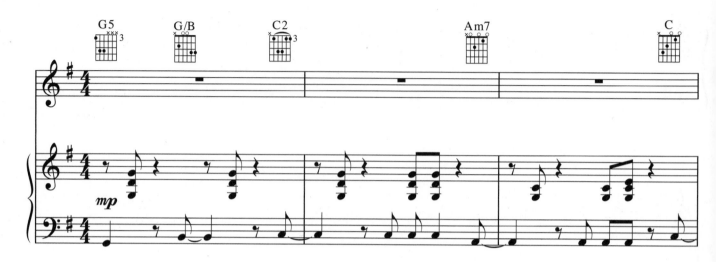

"More Than Words"
Lyrics and Music by
NUNO BETTENCOURT and GARY CHERONE

Say - in' "I___ love_____ you," is

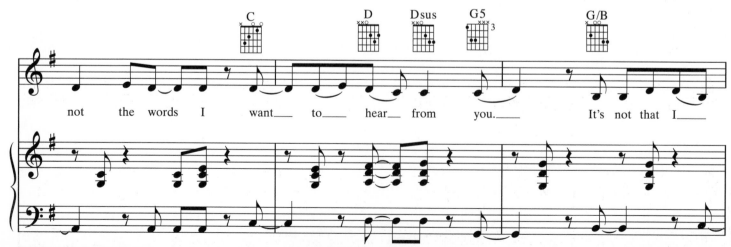

not the words I want__ to__ hear__ from you.___ It's not that I___

42

Freely
"Heaven"
Words and Music by
JANI LANE

Slow rock ballad ♩ = 76

col - or_____ deep in - side them like a blue sub - ur - ban sky._____ I don't

need to be the king of the___ world_____ as

long as I'm___ the he - ro of___ this lit - tle

girl._____ Oh,_____ yeah.___

44

Verse:

WANTED DEAD OR ALIVE

Words and Music by
JON BON JOVI
and RICHIE SAMBORA

Moderately slow rock ♩ = 76

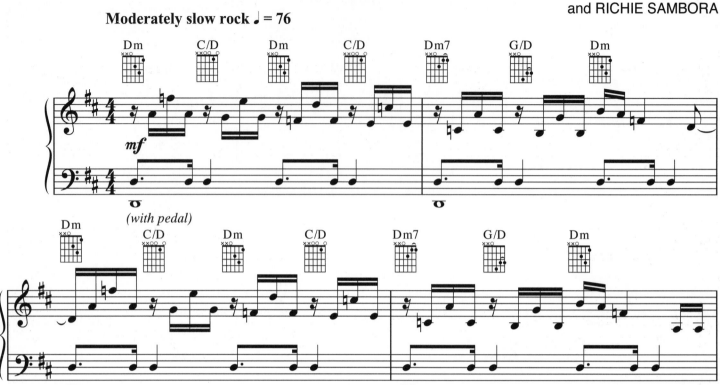

1. It's

Wanted Dead or Alive - 6 - 1

I WANT TO KNOW WHAT LOVE IS

Words and Music by
MICK JONES

*Originally recorded in G♭ major.

I Want to Know What Love Is - 5 - 1

Through the clouds I see love shine.
I've got no - where left to hide.

It keeps me
It looks like

Pre-Chorus:

warm as life grows cold - er.
love has fi - n'lly found me.

In my life, there's been

heart-ache and pain. I don't know if I can face it a - gain.

Can't stop now, I've trav - eled so far to change this lone - ly life.

POUR SOME SUGAR ON ME

Words and Music by
JOE ELLIOTT, PHIL COLLEN,
RICHARD SAVAGE, RICHARD ALLEN,
STEVE CLARK and ROBERT LANGE

Moderate rock ♩ = 86

1. Love is like a bomb, ba - by, come on, get it on.
2. Red light, yel - low light, green light, go.

Liv - in' like a lov - er with a ra - dar phone. Look - in' like a tramp, like a vi - de - o vamp.
Cra - zy lit - tle wom - an in a one-man show. Mir - ror queen, man - ne - quin, rhy - thm of love.

Dem - o - li - tion wom - an, can I be your man?
Sweet dream, sac - cha - rine, loos - en up.

You got - ta

Pour Some Sugar on Me - 6 - 1

60

HARDEN MY HEART

Words and Music by
MARVIN ROSS

Moderately bright rock shuffle ♩ = 132 (♫ = ♪ ♪)

Verse:

1. Cry-in' on the cor-ner, wait-in' in the rain,__ I swear__
2. All of my life I been wait-in' in the rain.__ I been

__ I'll nev-er ev-er wait__ a-gain.__ You gave me your word,_____ but
wait-in' for a feel-in' that nev-er ev-er came. It feels__ so close,_____ but

Harden My Heart - 3 - 1

64

Harden My Heart - 3 - 2

Harden My Heart - 3 - 3

SHADOWS OF THE NIGHT

Words and Music by
D.L. BYRON

Moderate rock ♩ = 120

We're run-nin' with the shad-ows of the night. So, ba-by, take my

hand, it-'ll be___ all right.___ Sur-ren-der all your dreams to me to-night.___

___ They'll come true in the end._____

Shadows of the Night - 5 - 1

70

HERE I GO AGAIN

Words and Music by
DAVID COVERDALE
and BERNIE MARSDEN

Moderately ♩ = 88

Verses 1 & 2:

1. I don't know where I'm go-ing, but I sure know where I've
2. Though I keep search-ing for an ans-wer, I nev-er seem to find what I'm look-

been.___ in___ songs of yes-ter-day,___
ing for. Oh Lord, I pray you give me___ strength to car-ry on.___

Hang-ing on the prom-is-es

72

CAN'T FIGHT THIS FEELING

Words and Music by
KEVIN CRONIN

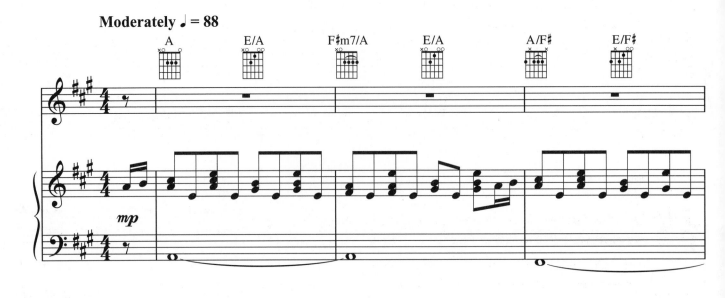

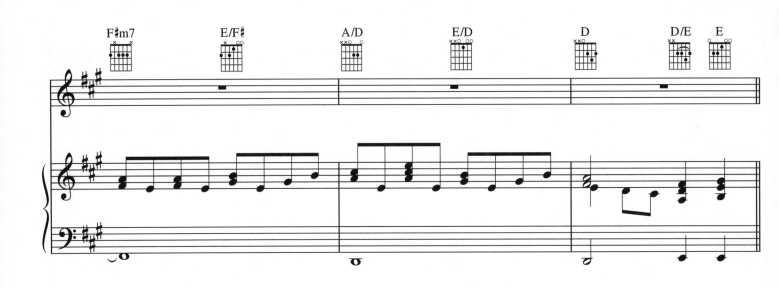

Verse 1:

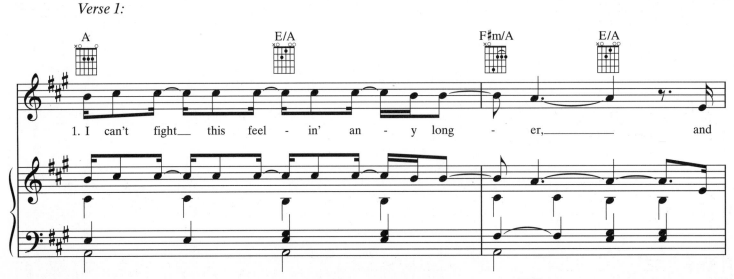

1. I can't fight___ this feel - in' an - y long - er,_____ and

ANY WAY YOU WANT IT

Words and Music by
NEAL SCHON and STEVE PERRY

Moderately fast ♩ = 138

An - y way you want it. That's the way you need it. An -

y way you want___ it.

Verse:

1. She loves to laugh.
2. I was a - lone,

She loves to sing.
I nev - er knew

She does ev - 'ry - thing.
what good love could do.

Any Way You Want It - 6 - 1

UNDERCOVER LOVE

Words and Music by
SAVAN KOTECHA, ADAM ANDERS
and PEER ASTROM

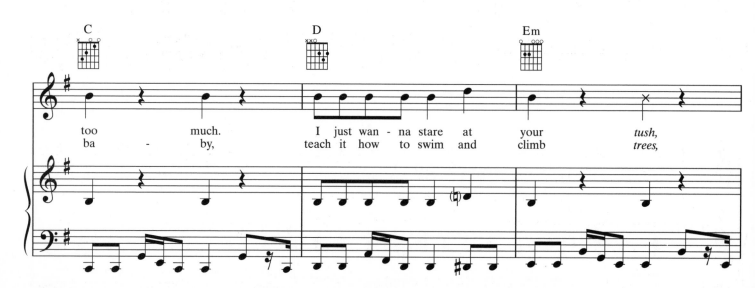

WE BUILT THIS CITY/ WE'RE NOT GONNA TAKE IT

Moderately bright rock ♩ = 152
"We Built This City"
Words and Music by
BERNIE TAUPIN, MARTIN PAGE,
DENNIS LAMBERT and PETER WOLF

We built this cit - y, we built this cit - y on

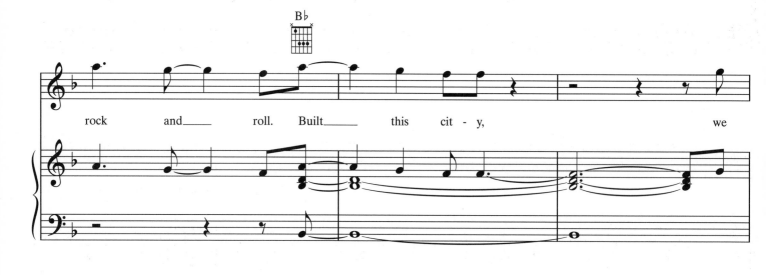

rock and roll. Built this cit - y, we

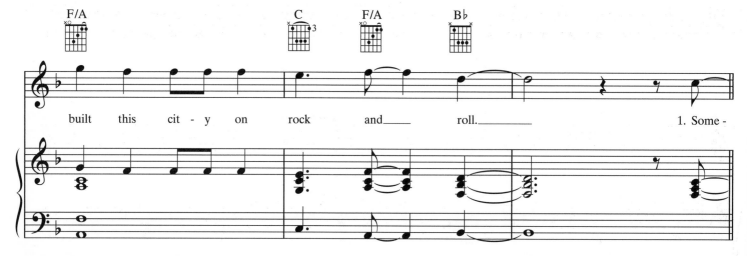

built this cit - y on rock and roll. 1. Some-

We Built This City / We're Not Gonna Take It - 7 - 1

Verse 1:

Verse 2:

DON'T STOP BELIEVIN'

Words and Music by
JONATHAN CAIN, NEAL SCHON
and STEVE PERRY

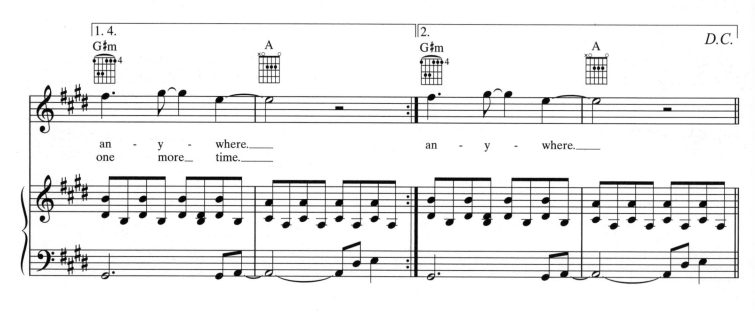

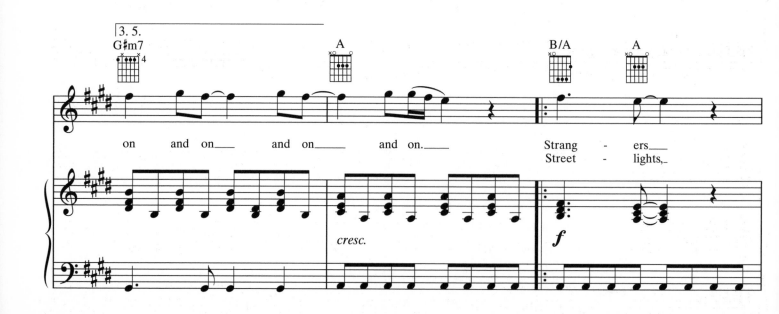